SPEEDY MACHINES
PLANES

Vic Parker

Illustrated by Tom Connell

Belitha Press

First published in the UK in 1999 by
Belitha Press Limited
London House, Great Eastern Wharf
Parkgate Road, London SW11 4NQ

Copyright © Belitha Press Ltd 1999
Text copyright © Vic Parker 1999

ISBN 1 84138 011 3

British Library Cataloguing in Publication Data for this book
is available from the British Library.

Printed in Singapore

Editor: Stephanie Bellwood
Designer: Helen James
Illustrator: Tom Connell
Consultant: Margaret Bellwood

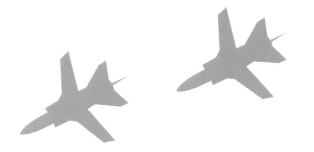

Contents

Up, up and away!

If you go on holiday by plane, you'll see that airliners are big enough to hold hundreds of people and their suitcases. What makes such huge, heavy machines faster than cars, boats and trains? Tiny fighter planes are even speedier. How do they zip across the sky almost too fast to see? This book will help you find out.

The back part of the plane is the **tail**. Panels in the tail move to help the plane climb (go up) or dive (go down).

The **rudder** is a part of the tail that moves right and left to turn the plane from side to side.

The **wings** of the plane have panels that move to make the aeroplane change direction. The panels are called **ailerons**.

The main body of the plane is called the **fuselage**.

The **pilot** flies the plane from a seat in the **cockpit**.

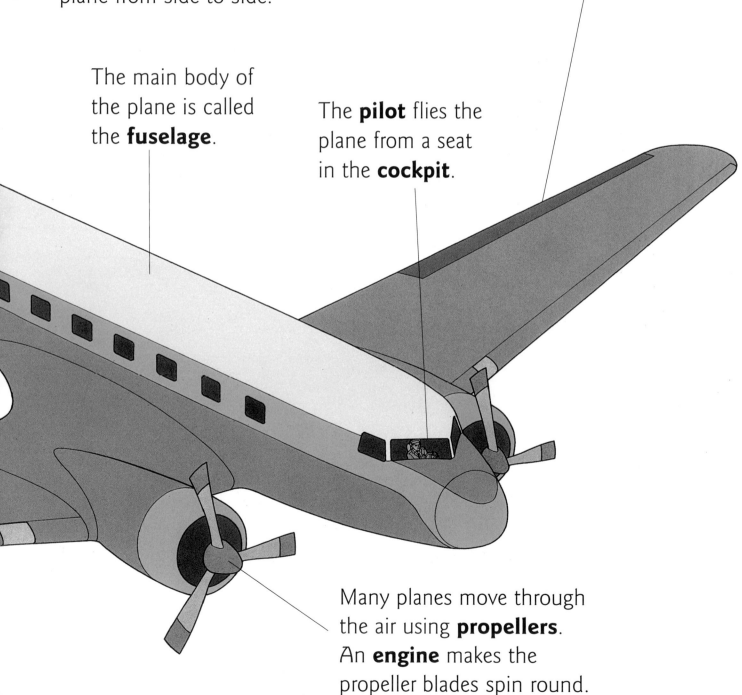

Many planes move through the air using **propellers**. An **engine** makes the propeller blades spin round.

Daring displays

These fighter
planes are part of
an exciting airshow.
The daredevil pilots
fly dangerously close to
one another, performing
loop-the-loops, nosedives and
other high-speed tricks. Way
down below on the ground, the
crowd gasps in amazement as the
fighters roar past, leaving trails
of coloured smoke across the sky.

Fast facts

Many planes are steered by hand, just like cars. Very fast aircraft have a computer that the pilot uses to control the plane.

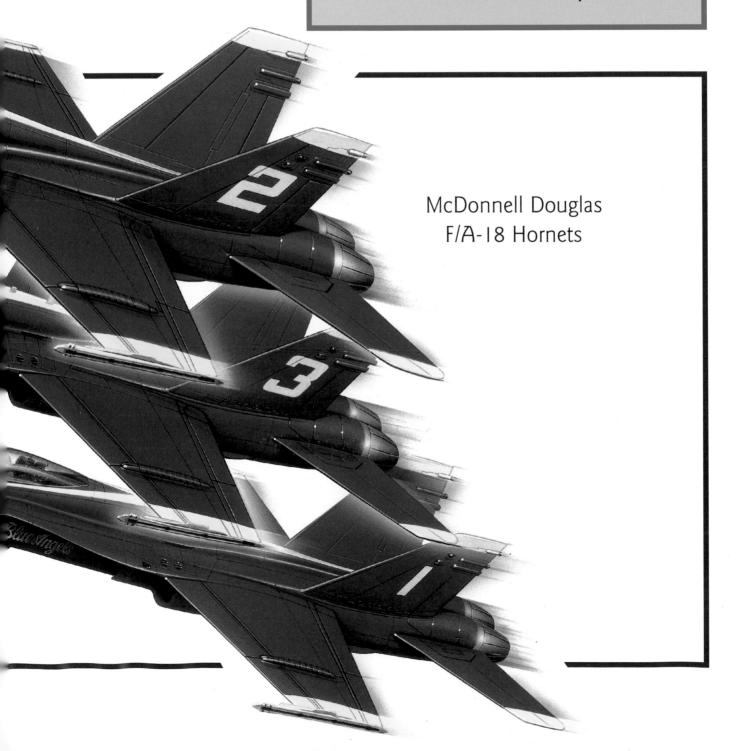

McDonnell Douglas
F/A-18 Hornets

Built for speed

Fast planes need to be long, slim and smooth so that they can slice through the air at top speed. Ideas for a new plane are drawn on computer. A model is made and tested to see how the real machine will fly. Finally the plane is built. Scientists and engineers all over the world are always trying to build better and faster aircraft.

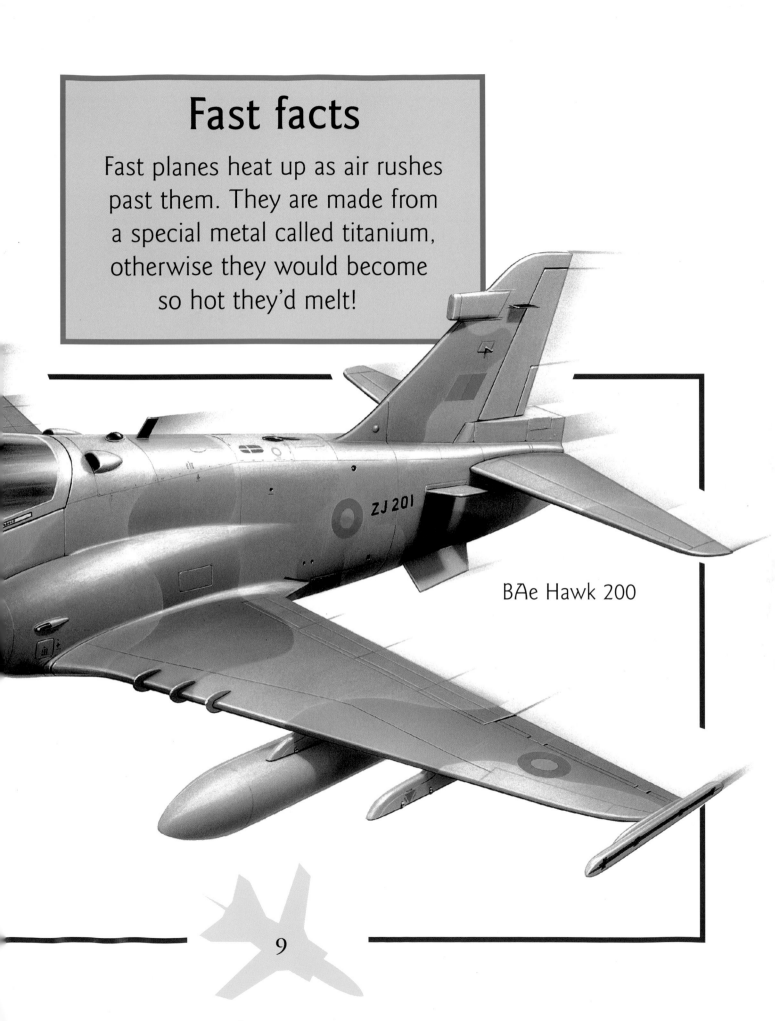

Fast facts

Fast planes heat up as air rushes past them. They are made from a special metal called titanium, otherwise they would become so hot they'd melt!

ZJ 201

BAe Hawk 200

On the wing

Slow planes, such as the Dash 7, have wings that stick straight out. Fast aeroplanes, such as the Boeing 767 jet airliner, are shaped like darts. They have slanted wings to help them cut through the air. The fastest planes of all, such as the Dassault Rafale fighter, have wings that are swept so far backwards that they become part of the tail. This design is called a delta wing.

Dash 7 airliner

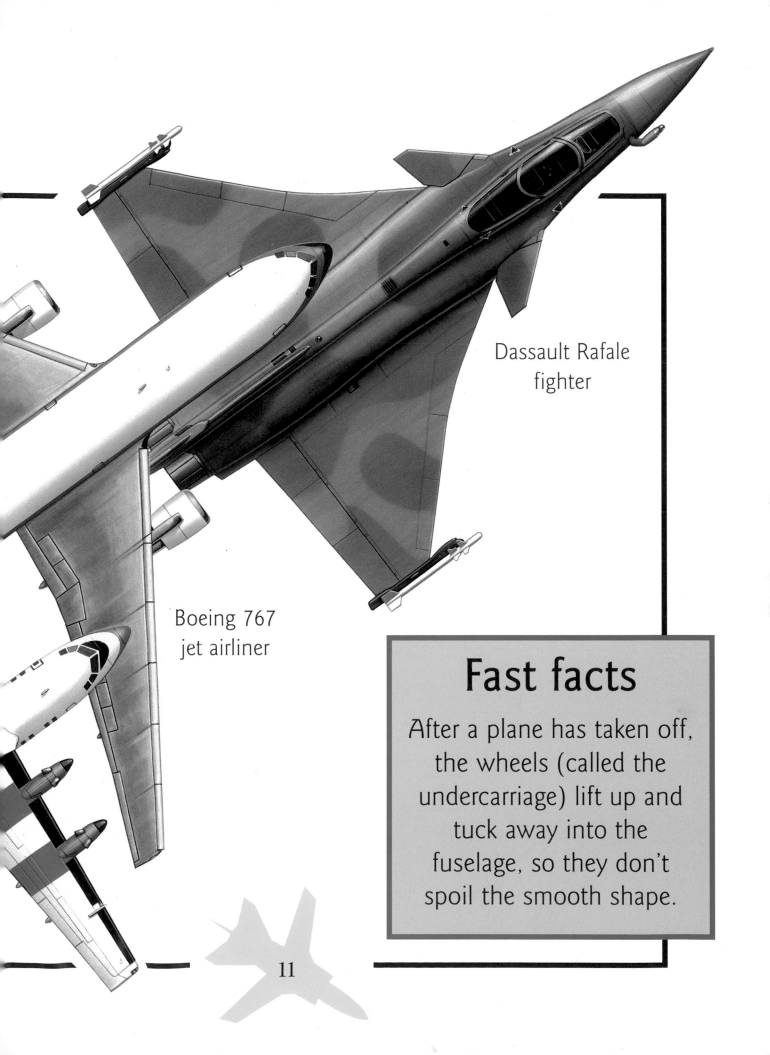

Dassault Rafale
fighter

Boeing 767
jet airliner

Fast facts

After a plane has taken off, the wheels (called the undercarriage) lift up and tuck away into the fuselage, so they don't spoil the smooth shape.

11

Jet power

Have you ever heard racing cars roar around a race track? Fast planes are even noisier because they are powered by fiery jet engines. Look at the hot gas blasting out of this Panavia Tornado as it takes off. The top speed for a small aircraft with an ordinary engine is 600 km/h, but an aircraft with a jet engine flies up to five times faster.

Fast facts

Aircraft with rocket engines are even more powerful than jet planes. Rocket planes go so fast and high that they can fly to where space begins.

Panavia Tornado

Planes of the past

Aeroplanes have been around for only 100 years. The very first planes were made of wood covered with cloth and they were slower than modern cars! The inventors of early aircraft did not have today's technology to help them, so their planes were often very dangerous and difficult to fly.

Fast facts

The Wright Flyer (1903) was the first plane. It flew at only 48 km/h. Ten years later the Spad 7 reached 210 km/h. Supermarine Spitfires used in the Second World War zoomed along at nearly 600 km/h.

Wright Flyer

Spad 7

Supermarine
Spitfire

Helicopter heroes

Helicopters don't need a runway to take off and land. Their long, thin blades whir round very fast, making enough wind to blow you over. These spinning blades lift the helicopter straight up into the air. Then the pilot tilts the blades and sends the helicopter speeding forwards.

Fast facts

The record for the fastest helicopter in the world is held by a British Westland Lynx. In 1986 it flew at a speed of 400 km/h.

Westland Lynx

Supersonic speed

Supersonic aircraft travel so amazingly fast that they are faster than the speed of sound! This means that they move faster than the time it takes for someone to speak and for you to hear what they say. Many top fighter planes can shoot through the sky at supersonic speeds.

Fast facts

The supersonic Eurofighter EFA 2000 has a talking computer that helps the pilot to find the way, or navigate. The pilot speaks to the computer and it answers back!

Eurofighter EFA 2000

Jumbo jets

The largest passenger planes in the world are Boeing 747s. These planes are nicknamed jumbo jets because they are the elephants of the skies! The first jumbo jets were built around 30 years ago. Newer Boeing 747-400 planes are even more powerful. They carry up to 566 passengers at a time, from one side of the world to the other without stopping.

Boeing 747 Jumbo Jet

Fast facts

In 1991 a Boeing 747 carried the most passengers ever recorded on one airliner. It flew 1,088 people from Ethiopia to Israel – including two babies born during the flight!

21

Amazing airliners

Concorde is the fastest airliner in the world. It has a pointed nose called a droop snoot. The nose tips down when the plane takes off and lands so that the pilot can see the ground below. Engineers are now putting the finishing touches to an exciting new supersonic airliner that will go twice as fast as Concorde.

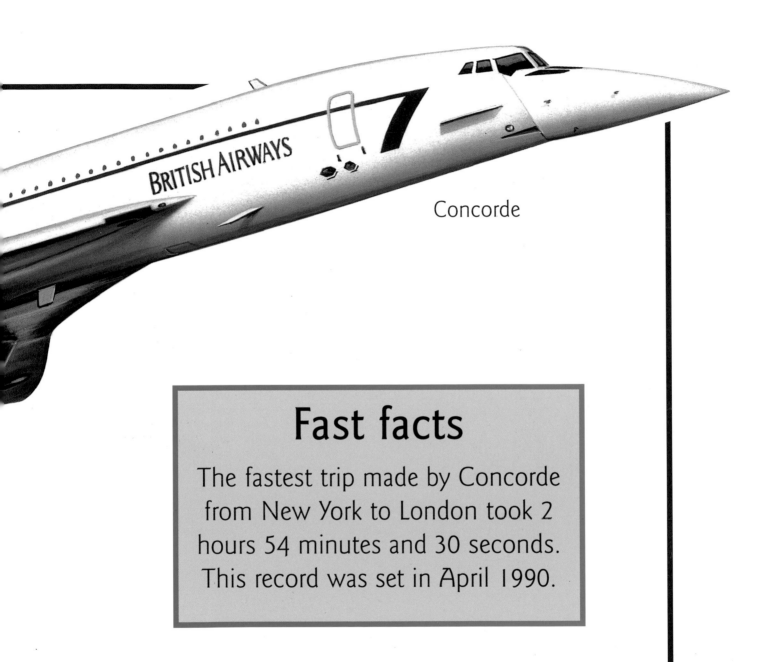

Concorde

Fast facts

The fastest trip made by Concorde from New York to London took 2 hours 54 minutes and 30 seconds. This record was set in April 1990.

Spies in the skies

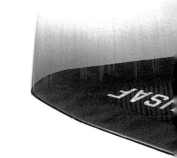

Supersonic spy planes are used to carry out top secret missions. They sneak speedily into enemy air space and slip out again without being noticed. This Lockheed SR-71 can fly so fast that its wings heat up to 430°C, which is about eight times as hot as the hottest desert in the world.

Fast facts

A Lockheed SR-71 set an air speed record in 1976 that has never been beaten. It flew at 3,529 km/h.

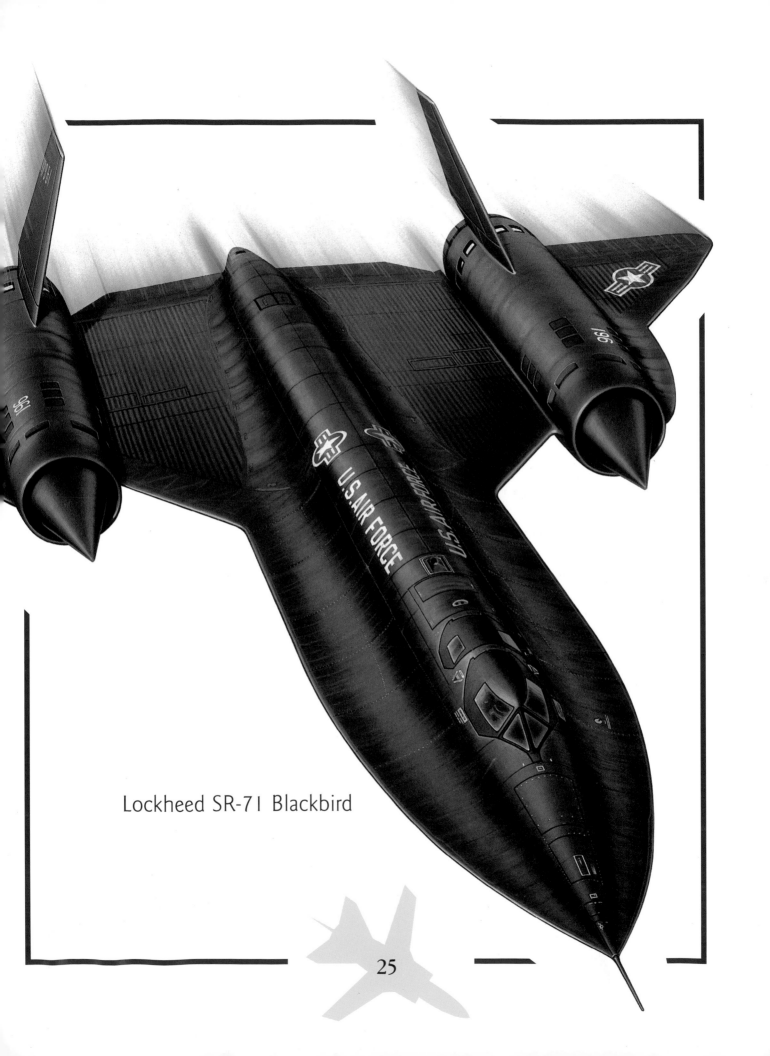

Lockheed SR-71 Blackbird

25

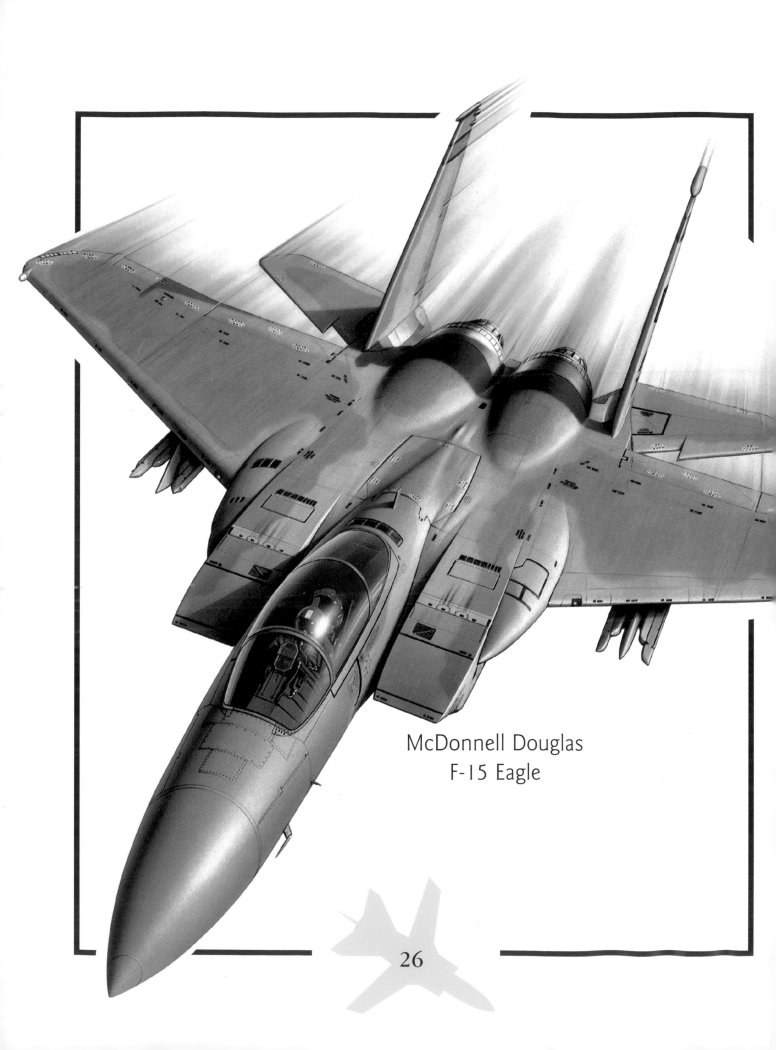

McDonnell Douglas
F-15 Eagle

Fast fighters

Fighter planes are the fastest aircraft of all. They are so small that only one or two people can squeeze into the tiny cockpit, but they have huge, powerful engines. Fighters dart all over the skies to attack or escape from an enemy. They can even zoom straight upwards, like space rockets.

Fast facts

Some fighters have swing-wings. These special wings stick out straight for take-off and landing, then swivel backwards when the plane travels at supersonic speeds.

Air racers

Old planes are just as much fun as brand new aircraft. If you visit an airshow you can watch fighter planes from the Second World War racing each other. The planes are specially rebuilt, but they look just as they did years ago. It's easy to imagine these little planes dive-bombing and fighting in high-speed air battles, then turning and racing for home.

Fast facts

The first long-distance air race from England to Australia was in 1934. The winner was a de Havilland Comet. The journey took almost three days and nights.

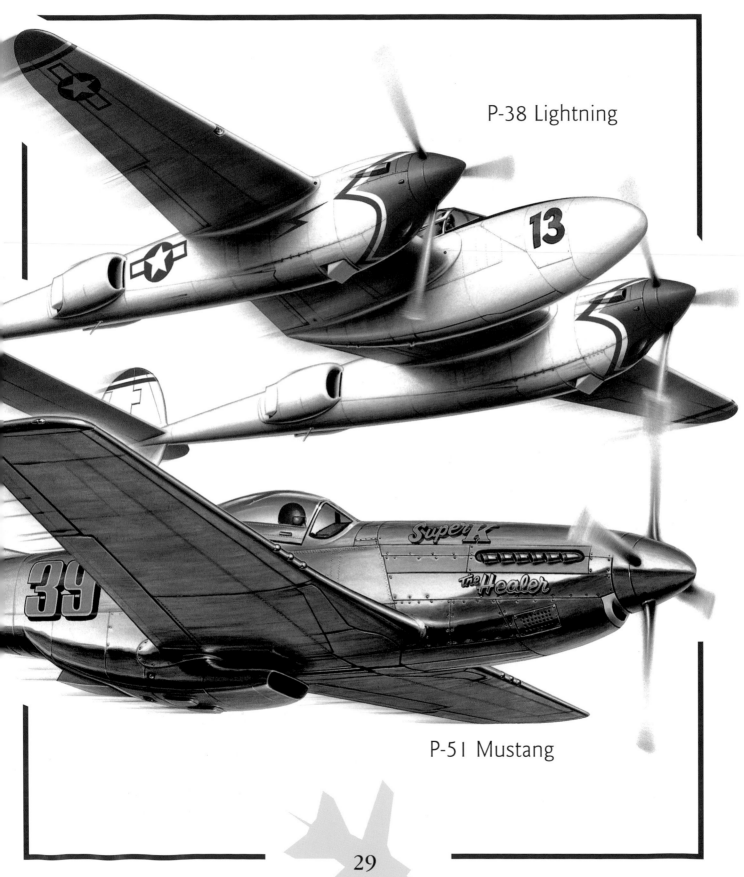

P-38 Lightning

P-51 Mustang

29

Blast off!

The US space shuttle looks like a jet plane, but it has some very special differences. Five rocket engines thrust it into the sky and out into space. It blasts through space at more than 40,000 km/h, then comes back to land on a runway, just like an airliner. Who knows – one day a space shuttle might take you to the moon or to explore more distant planets.

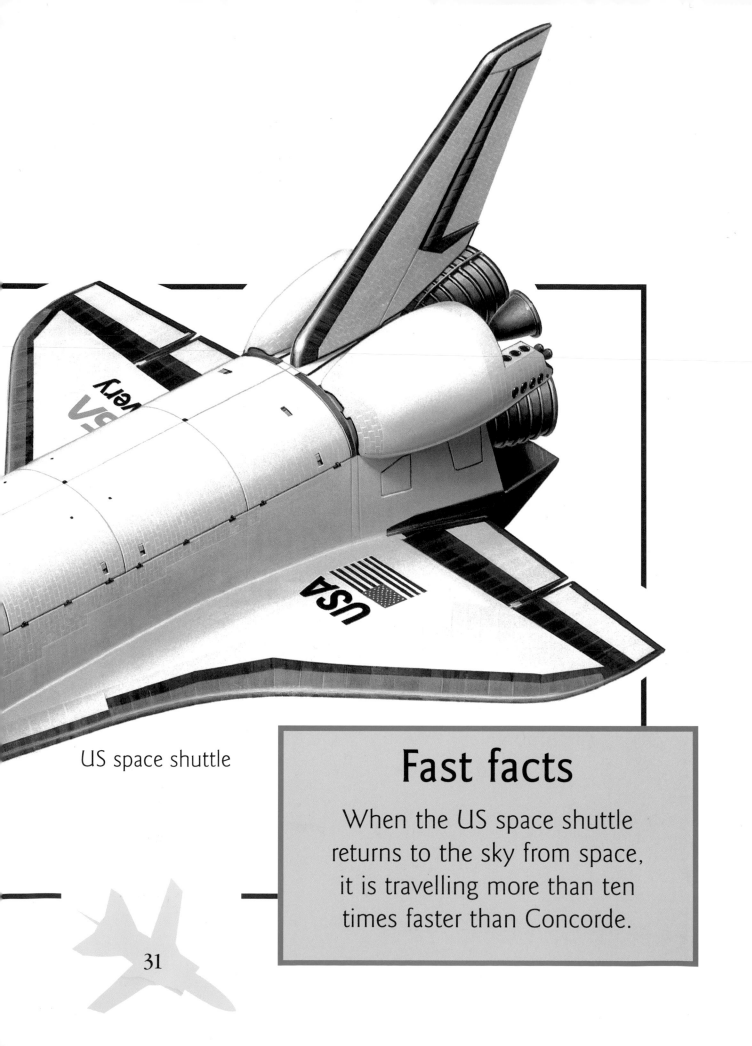

US space shuttle

Fast facts

When the US space shuttle returns to the sky from space, it is travelling more than ten times faster than Concorde.

Index